NOTE TO PARENTS

This familiar Bible story has been retold in a sensitive and simple way so that young children can read and understand it for themselves. But the special message of the story remains unchanged. It is the message of God's love and care for us all.

The Boy with the Loaves and Fishes

retold by Marjorie Newman
illustrated by Edgar Hodges

Copyright © 1990 World International Publishing Ltd.
All rights reserved.
Published in Great Britain by World International Publishing Ltd.,
an Egmont Company, Egmont House, PO Box 111, Great Ducie Street,
Manchester M60 3BL.
Printed in Germany.
ISBN 0 7235 4465 4
Reprinted 1992

A catalogue record for this book is available from the British Library

It was an early morning in Galilee, in the Bible lands. A boy came running out of his house. He wanted to catch some fish! He knew a special place to try. Sometimes the fish lay there . . .

Carefully, he scrambled out over the rocks. He peered down. Yes! There they were! . . . He slid in his hands and – *GRAB*! He'd caught a fish for breakfast! . . . Try again . . . Another! . . . But they were quite small. Could he catch more?

No. However much he tried, he could only catch those two fish. Sadly, he walked towards his house. Some of his friends went by.
"Have a good breakfast!" they laughed.

The boy took no notice. His mother didn't laugh. She put the fish to bake on the fire. But just as they were ready for him to eat, the boy heard something!

People were hurrying past the house. Some of the boy's friends were there.

"Hey!" they called. "Jesus is up on the hillside! We're going to see Him!"

"Mum!" cried the boy. "Can I go too?"

"What about breakfast?" said his mother.
"Please can I take the food with me?" he begged.
"All right," said his mother. Quickly she packed the fish, and some loaves. "Stay with the people from this town!" she reminded him.

The boy hurried along the hillside path with the others. Now there were crowds of people, all going to see Jesus.

At last they reached the place where He was. The boy and his friends managed to get to the front.

"That's Jesus!" one of the grown-ups pointed out. "And those men with Him are His disciples. His special helpers."

Then Jesus began to speak. The crowd was quiet, listening carefully.

All day Jesus spoke. He talked about God, the loving Father. He told wonderful stories. And He healed the sick. The day went by.

Late in the afternoon, the boy suddenly felt hungry. He'd been so busy listening, he'd forgotten about eating! So had everyone else!

The boy started to unpack his food. Then he heard Jesus' disciples say, "Master! It will soon be dark. The people are tired. And they've had nothing to eat. Send them away now. Then they can buy food in the nearby villages."

Jesus answered, "*You* feed them."

"But it would cost eight months' wages to buy enough for them all!" cried Philip, one of the disciples.

The boy looked at Jesus. He thought about the hungry people.

Then the boy looked around. No one else seemed to have any food. But *his* fish – the fish *he* had caught – could he bear to share them . . .? Besides, he was very hungry. In any case, would they be any use?

He looked down at the two small fish. He remembered how his friends had laughed. Perhaps Jesus would laugh, too . . .

The boy looked again at Jesus. No, Jesus wouldn't laugh . . .

Shyly, the boy went forward. Timidly, he touched Andrew, another of the disciples. "Here is some food!" he said.

Andrew smiled at the boy. He took him to Jesus. "Master!" he said. "There is a boy here with five barley loaves and two small fishes!" Then he sighed. "What use is that among so many?"

The boy held his breath.

But, smiling, Jesus accepted the boy's gift. He said to His disciples, "Tell everyone to sit down!" There were about five thousand people!

When at last everyone was seated, Jesus said a thank you prayer to God for the loaves and fishes.

Then Jesus began to divide the food. He gave it to the disciples to take round.

The boy watched, his eyes wide. There was going to be enough for everybody!

Now the people were laughing, and talking — and eating! Jesus and His disciples and the boy ate, too. And when everybody had had enough, Jesus' disciples collected up *twelve baskets* of scraps!

The boy could hardly believe it ! But he was very happy.

It was nearly dark now. The boy set out for home with the other people from his town. He couldn't wait to get back.

He rushed indoors. "Mum! Mum!" he cried. "Listen!" And he told her the whole story.